WATCHMAN NEE

Expecting the Lord's Blessing

Living Stream Ministry
Anaheim, CA • www.lsm.org

ISBN 978-1-57593-862-2

Living Stream Ministry
2431 W. La Palma Ave., Anaheim, CA 92801
P. O. Box 2121, Anaheim, CA 92814 USA

Printed in India

14 15 16 17 18 / 9 8 7 6 5 4

EXPECTING THE LORD'S BLESSING

Of late a thought has been constantly with me that all the work is dependent on God's blessing. Often we are faithful, but despite our faithfulness there is no blessing and no fruit. Often we are diligent, but despite our diligence there is no blessing and no fruit. Often we exercise our faith; we truly believe God can do something. We also pray that He would work, but everything is in vain when God does not bless us. Sooner or later, we who serve God must be brought to the point of expecting God's blessing. Without God's blessing, our faithfulness, diligence, faith, and prayers will be to no avail. However, if we have God's blessing, there will be fruit even if we seem to be wrong or hopeless. Therefore, all problems are a matter of God's blessing.

ONE

I would like to bring out the matter of multiplying the five loaves (Mark 6:35-44;

8:1-9) with respect to God's blessing. It is not a matter of how many loaves we have in our hands, but whether or not God has blessed them. Even if we had more than five loaves, this would not be enough to feed four or five thousand people. Even if we had ten times or even one hundred times more, we still would not have enough to feed four or five thousand people. It is not a matter of how much we have. Sooner or later, we must be brought to the point of seeing that it is not a matter of what we can pull out of our storage shed, nor is it a matter of how great our gift is or how much power we have. The day must come in which we say to the Lord, "Everything depends on Your blessing. When I bring the loaves before You, whether there are one or two of them or one hundred, Lord, still everything depends on Your blessing." This is a basic matter. How much blessing has the Lord really given us? It does not really matter how many loaves there are. The Lord's blessing nourishes people and gives them life.

One matter is troubling my heart: Do we truly treasure God's blessing? This is a basic question concerning the work. Perhaps we do not even have five loaves today, but our need is greater than four thousand or five thousand people. I am afraid that we have less in our storehouse than the apostles, but our need is greater than the need at the time of the apostles. Our own store, source, power, labor, and faithfulness will be manifest one day that they are useless to us. Brothers, our future holds great disappointment for us because we will see that we can do nothing.

We must notice something in the Gospels. Why does the Lord do two miracles that are almost the same in nature and in action? I am afraid it is because this lesson is not easy to learn. Why does He feed the five thousand and then feed the four thousand? Two miracles of almost identical nature are repeated twice in the Gospels. We must learn this lesson, but it is not easy. Many people still do not look to God's blessing, but instead look at the few loaves in their own hands! The loaves in our hands are so pitifully few, but we still base our plans on them. The more we plan in this way, however, the harder the work becomes. Sometimes it becomes impossible. I am somewhat comforted by the words spoken by a brother one hundred years ago. He said, "When the Lord wants to work a small miracle, He puts me in a difficult situation. When He wants to work a great miracle, He puts me in an impossible situation." Our situation is difficult, and it even seems impossible. Many times it is really hard, and we are like the little boy with just a few loaves. We can only hope for a miracle, and this miracle is the Lord Himself taking them up and blessing them.

Brothers and sisters, the miracles are produced by the Lord's blessing. His blessing changes and multiplies the loaves. When we do not see anything, when there is no assurance, when the situation is impossible, His blessing multiplies the loaves. The miracles are based on the Lord's blessing. When there is a blessing, five thousand or four thousand people are fed. Without a blessing, even two hundred or five hundred denarii worth of bread are not enough to satisfy that many people. The Lord was training the disciples, bringing them to the point of looking to Him for His blessing.

Many times we do not have the capacity to do something. The outward environment is difficult, even impossible. If our eyes are fixed on the circumstances, we will not have any way to deal with them. However, the Lord repeatedly brings us through. These times are the Lord's blessing. When we have blessing, everything goes well and nothing is difficult. Without the Lord's blessing, everything goes wrong and nothing is easy. The Lord wants to bring us to a point where His blessing takes the first place, a point where we have never been. When the Lord brings us to such a point, He will have a way to go on. If the Lord does not bring us to this point, we will have to say that even two hundred denarii worth of bread is not enough. Today the problem is that we cannot meet the need in ourselves. All of our money combined is not enough. All of us combined is insufficient, but the Lord has a way. In the Lord's work, the basic problem is the Lord's blessing; nothing else matters.

TWO

Brothers, if God brings us to the point of seeing that everything in God's work depends upon His blessing, it will bring about a basic change in our labor for God. We would not consider how many people, how much money, or how much bread we have. We would say we do not have enough, but the blessing is sufficient. The blessing meets the need that we cannot meet. Although we cannot measure up to the size of the need, the blessing is greater than our lack. When we see this, the work will have a basic change. In every matter we must look at the blessing more than we consider the situation. Methods, considerations, human wisdom, and clever words are all useless. In God's work we should believe in and expect His blessing. Many times we are careless and damage the work, but this is not a problem. If the Lord gives us a small blessing, we can get through any problem.

We truly hope that we would not make mistakes or speak and act loosely in the work. When we have the Lord's blessing, however, it seems that we cannot err even when we are wrong. Sometimes it seems that we have made a serious mistake, but with God's blessing the result is not really an error. I once said to Brother Witness that if we had the Lord's blessing, the things we did right would be right and the things we did wrong would be right as well. Nothing could damage the blessing.

THREE

The basic concern today is that we must

learn to live in a way that does not hinder God's blessing. Some habits force God to withhold His blessing, and these must be eliminated. Some temperaments keep God from blessing, and these must be done away with. We must learn to believe in God's blessing, rely on it, and eliminate the barriers that prevent us from receiving it.

Let us take Sian as an example. When the brothers were divided into two parties, this definitely hindered God from blessing. If their problem had continued to exist, God's blessing would not have come in. In another example, there have been some difficulties in Szechuan recently. Therefore, we cannot expect Szechuan to have any special blessing. I merely mention these matters as examples.

We must see that the Lord withholds no good thing from us. If the work is not going well, if the brothers and sisters are in a poor condition, or if the number of saved ones is not increasing, we should not use the environment or certain people as an excuse. We cannot blame the brothers. I am afraid that the real reason lies with our harboring of some frustrations to the blessing. If the Lord can get through in us, the Lord's blessing will be greater than our capacity. Once God said to the Israelites, "Prove Me, if you will, by this,... whether I will open to you the windows of heaven and pour out blessing for you until there is no room for it" (Mal. 3:10). God is still saying this today. The normal life of a Christian is a life of blessing, and the normal work of a Christian is a work of blessing. If we do not receive blessing, we should say, "Lord, perhaps I am the problem."

With the passing years it becomes more and more evident that some brothers receive God's blessing while others do not. Of ourselves, we are not able to form any judgment about this matter, but over the years this fact has become so evident that we know beforehand that there will be fruit if one brother goes out but none if another brother goes out. We seemingly can forecast the result.

FOUR

There are definite requirements for receiving the Lord's blessing. It does not come by accident or luck. God has His ways and works according to His principles. God likes certain conditions and does not like others. Esau was very good, but God did not like him. Jacob was not good, but God liked him. God has His own reasons. If a person does not receive God's blessing, there is a reason for it. If we do not receive God's blessing, we should not push the responsibility for it onto the situation or environment. There is always a reason for not being blessed. If we could be brought to the point in which we wholeheartedly hope for His blessing and wholeheartedly ask Him to show us the reason for not being blessed, God's work would have a great future. I really hope that we could live on the earth by expecting the Lord's blessing. Nothing is as important as God's blessing. The results of the work are in the blessing.

I am well aware that we all have our own particular weaknesses. God seems to overlook some of these, but He will not tolerate other ones. Where these exist His blessing cannot rest. It seems that God does not care about some weaknesses. It does not bother Him if you make these mistakes over and over again, but God cares about other weaknesses very much. Therefore, we must be very careful about the weaknesses which might cause us to lose God's blessing. We may be unable to eliminate all our weaknesses, but we must ask God to have mercy on us so that we would be those who are able to receive His blessing. We should say to the Lord, "This vessel is weak, but forbid that it should be too shallow or too small to contain Your blessing." Even though we are shallow and small, we are still able to contain His blessing. God's blessing and gifts are His work. Thus, we hope God would have mercy on us.

FIVE

Oh, that blessing might flow from us as it flowed from Abraham. I believe that there will soon be a great turn in the gospel work. May the Lord bless us and have mercy on us. May we regard blessing as if we were accustomed to receiving it constantly. We do not want to frustrate God from blessing us greatly. The salvation of one thousand people may hinder the salvation of tens of thousands. Perhaps the salvation of a few score people in one place is a hindrance to the salvation of several thousand others. Each time we receive one blessing, we should expect to receive a second blessing. We must continuously step into greater blessings from God. Each of our co-workers must look to God to do a work among us such as He has never done before. Immediately before us lies a work that is ten times greater, even one hundred times greater, than that which is behind us. Is it possible that the few people who have been saved and the meeting-hall we have built have become the limits of our blessing? In the past the work constantly grew, but now we have tied it up. Our past blessings have become our present frustrations. This is very pitiful.

Each time we come before God, we must be like we were the first time we came out to work. Some have been working for twenty years, yet they seem like those who are new to the work. Some have been working for thirty years, but they seem like they are new in the work. We must set the things of the past aside. In difficult situations God will do more if our hopes, expectations, and hearts are large. We must never measure God by our capacity. A few loaves of bread can feed four or five thousand people. If the blessing is large, nothing can hinder it. If we who serve the Lord truly look for God's blessing when we gather together, the future results will be more than we can ask or think.

SIX

God's blessing is like a bird that will only fly from the outside into a room by itself. When it is at the window, we cannot call it to come in. If it comes in, however, it is very easy to chase away. God will bless what He wants to bless; we cannot force Him to do anything. Like the bird, it is difficult to lure in and easy to chase away. With just a little carelessness, we can chase the blessing away.

Over the past two or three years, I have observed our co-workers doing many things. One co-worker said something to another co-worker, and they had an argument. He was absolutely right in what he said and did, but in my heart, I wanted to say, "Brother, you are right, but should we behave according to right and wrong? Or should we behave according to what will bring in God's blessing?" We often may do something right, but what can we do if God does not bless us when we do things right? We should not ask whether our every action is right or wrong. Instead, we should ask whether we have God's blessing.

12

We are not here to argue about right and wrong; we are here to ask God to bless us. Seeking God's blessing on our work will limit us much in our speaking and in our daily living. We may be right, but will God bless us? It is very easy for us to cut off our blessing. It is also very easy to cut off the blessing of others as well. Our standard is not right or wrong. We look for God's blessing. Both may be right, but can God bless such a work? Our lives must be governed by God's blessing.

In God's work He will not bless what is wrong, but He will not bless what is right either. When we stand together in one accord, the blessing comes. Therefore, I want us to know that it is a very serious matter when the brothers argue with each other. We may be absolutely right in the matter, but the blessing will stop! Brothers, let me solemnly warn about speaking loosely or thinking that it is good enough just to be right. May the Lord have mercy on us. The brothers have to be careful about speaking among themselves and criticizing one another. It does not matter if we are right. If we are right and God does not bless us, what is the use of being right? The work is not built upon our abilities, nor is it built upon our gifts, faithfulness, or labor. If we miss God's blessing, everything is finished.

SEVEN

What is blessing? Blessing is God working without any cause. Logically speaking, one penny should buy one penny's worth of goods. But sometimes, without spending a cent, God gives us ten thousand pennies' worth of goods. This means that what we have received is beyond reckoning. God's blessing is any work He performs without cause. This work surpasses what we should receive. Five loaves fed five thousand people, and there were still twelve full baskets left over! This is blessing. Some people should not get a certain kind of result. They should only have a little, but surprisingly they have much. Our entire work is built upon God's blessing. The blessing is the result of receiving what we do not deserve, that is, the result of receiving beyond what our gift warrants us to receive. The result that we get, which is beyond what our strength earns, is the blessing. Putting it more strongly, we do not deserve any results because of our weaknesses and failures, but astoundingly we obtain something, and what we obtain is the blessing. If we look for God's blessing, He will give us unexpected results. In our service do we hope for God to give us great results? Many brothers and sisters only look for results that can be expected from themselves alone. Blessing means that the result is not in proportion to the cause.

If we only look for results based on what we are, if we only look for a little fruit, and if we do not hope for great results, we run the risk of losing God's blessing. Since we only pay attention to the fact that we are laboring night and day, God cannot do anything beyond our expectation. We must put ourselves in a position in which God can bless us. We must say to the Lord, "Based on what we are, we should not obtain any results, but, Lord, for the sake of Your name, Your church, and Your way, we hope You will give something to us." Having faith in the work is believing and expecting God's blessing. In God's work, having faith means having the conviction that the result will not be in proportion to us. When we practice this, I believe God will bless our way. I hope that as the brothers discuss the matter of the migrations, the Lord's blessing will exceed our expectation.

At times it seems that God not only grants no blessing, but even deliberately withholds it. For God to withhold His blessing is more serious than for Him to not grant blessing. With our strength and gifts, we should have better results, but we do not obtain them. We labor through the night and should obtain certain results, but if God withholds His blessing, we will obtain less than we should. We labor for a long time but obtain no fruit. We are diligent, yet there are no results. This is what happens when God withholds His blessing.

I wonder if we feel the seriousness of this. We absolutely must not argue about the right way to do things. Being right is of no use. We must pay attention to whether or not God blesses us. Often we are very right, yet God does not bless us. It is right to fish all night, yet God does not bless us. We do not live on earth by doing what is right; we live to experience God's blessing. David and Abraham both made mistakes, Isaac was not very useful, and Jacob was crafty, but God blessed them all. It is not a matter of being right or wrong, but of being blessed by

God. Perhaps we who are here today are much better than Jacob, but if God does not bless us, nothing will avail. We must be those who can be blessed by God. We can argue and be right, but it is useless if God does not bless us.

The entire future of the work depends on God's blessing, not on being right. If God blesses, then many sinners will be saved. If God blesses, we will be able to send people out to the remote regions. If there is no blessing, people will not get saved. If there is no blessing, workers will not be produced. If there is no blessing, no one will offer anything. If there is no blessing, no one will migrate. When the blessing is here, even things that seem wrong are right. When God blesses, we cannot go wrong even if we try. One time there was a meeting in which it seemed that we sang the wrong hymn, but we had a good result because we had God's blessing. Sometimes when we preach, it seems that we are speaking the wrong word to the wrong audience, but God still blesses some in the audience. When we speak again, we still may speak the wrong word, but God blesses another group of people. I am not saying that we can be loose intentionally. I am saying that we cannot go wrong when we have God's blessing. It seems that our mistakes should be a frustration, but He cannot be hindered. God said, "Jacob have I loved, but Esau have I hated" (Rom. 9:13). God blesses whom He likes. This is a very serious matter. We should not think that the blessing is a small thing. The blessing is souls and consecrated people. Behind the word *blessing* perhaps there are fifty souls or one hundred consecrations. The words, attitudes, and opinions of certain people can stop the Lord's blessing. We must ask the Lord to prick us inwardly until we obtain His blessing. If we do not do this, our sin of losing the Lord's blessing will be greater than any other sin. The blessing could be hundreds or thousands of souls. We must look to God for the blessing and not let it escape. We must beg God to give us grace.

EIGHT

O brothers! We must learn to live in God's blessing. It is good to work and do things, but we must have our capacity increased. We must ask God to keep us in His blessing in our work and actions. If we do not resolve this problem, our work will be severely damaged. Brother Witness was in Shanghai in 1945. One day he said that the brothers' meeting experienced great blessing from God. I believe that Brother Witness has made some progress in this matter. We must come before God to see that we do not expect the results of our labor, but expect God's blessing. Sometimes there are some results from our work, but they are dry and poor. If we expect God's blessing, many things will happen that are beyond our expectation. If we wait upon God's blessing, things will happen beyond our capacity. We must continually look for miracles and unexpected occurrences in the work. We should not keep expecting that we will be able to bear any fruit. Our expectation of that small amount of fruit limits God. If we do not expect God's blessing, there is not much hope for our future. We will have financial difficulties, and it will be difficult for us to go on. Therefore, we should not look for results commensurate with our individual labor, but we should look for God's blessing. If we only look for commensurate results, I do not know how many years it will take for many people to believe in the Lord. We must always look for God to do things beyond our expectations. We must ask God to give us the vision to see the meaning of blessing.

Some are checking to see whether or not the young people are doing things right. Instead, we should be checking to see if a person is being blessed by God. If a person can be blessed by God, we do not know how much more fruit he will bear beyond just his gift and ability. If he does not have the blessing, his carefulness and labor will be in vain.

Some people are blessed by God, and other people are not blessed by God. We may have a better temper and a larger gift than a certain brother, but he bears fruit in his work, while we cannot bear fruit in ours. We look down on many people because we are better, yet God blesses them. We cannot say that God is wrong. We must realize that before God, we are those whom He cannot bless.

We should not become angry or jealous about this matter. Instead, we should judge ourselves soberly. We have many excuses, and so do our brothers. We are right, and so are they. But what can we do if God does not bless? We are right, but we cannot win souls. They are right, but the church is not built up. We are right, but it is in vain. Therefore, we must eliminate all the things that stop and frustrate the blessing. From now on we should not be those who stubbornly argue over right and wrong; we must be those who receive great blessings from God.